THE BIBLE GOD'S WORD TO US

Enlarged Print Edition

Gerald M. Overall

The Bible
God's Word To Us

Copyright © 2021 Gerald M. Overall

ISBN-9798768340520

Table of Contents

Introduction

There are billions of believers in Christ Jesus today. And every one of them will tell you it's God's word to us that led them to this belief. Yet if you ask most Christians today where the Bible came from, most could not tell you. We believe that God so loved the world that He gave His one and only Son so that through faith in Him, we might not perish but live forever. And we can tell you where that is in our Bible. But the question is, how did we get our Bible in the first place. And can we trust in it?

At the time of Jesus' death, burial, resurrection, and ascension back to heaven, the 66 books Bible had not been compiled yet. All the writers of the New Testament died by AD 100, and the Bible still had not been complied into the 66 books we have today. The compilation of the sixty-six books we have today would not happen until 397 AD. In this book, we will look at the events that led to creating the Bible we have today. We need to, as Christians, be able to intelligently and accurately answer those who question the validity of God's word today. Our salvation depends on whether the Bible is God's word to us or not. If not, then we are not saved.

Let me say that I believe every word in the Bible from Genesis 1:1 to Revelation 22:21 is the inspired word of God. God's word says this to us in 2nd Timothy 3:16-17, and again in 2nd Peter 1:20-21, and by faith, I believe Him. Both Paul and Peter, inspired by the Holy Spirit, tell us in their letters that the Bible is, in fact, God's word to us. Paul tells us that all scripture is God-breathed and is given to us by God for instruction in righteousness and to show us how to live for Jesus Christ while we are here in this world serving Him. Peter reminds us that the Holy Spirit moved those prophets of old, and they spoke as the Holy Spirit carried them along and not from themselves. The Lord says to us in the letter to the Hebrews that "it is impossible to please Him without faith" and "if anyone comes to Him, they must believe He exists and that He rewards those who sincerely seek Him." (See Hebrews 11:6) So we must believe for ourselves that the word of God is, in fact, His word to us.

I am not writing this book to prove to anyone that the Bible is the word of God. Only faith in the death, burial, and resurrection of Jesus Christ can do that. The Bible teaches that without the Holy Spirit, it is impossible to know what the word of God is saying to us. (See John 3:5-6 and 1st Corinthians 2:9-16) There is no need for me to attempt to prove the validity of God's word because the word of God provides proof that its origins are from The Lord our God Himself, the creator of the heavens and the earth. (See Romans 1:18-20) All we have to do is speak it and live it out by faith. And Jesus will do the rest. (see Luke 24:45)

So having said that, what I am going to do is trace the Bible back to its humble beginnings. My purpose is to educate those who have placed their faith in the risen Christ. I firmly believe every Christian needs to know the history of the Bible, that they have put their trust in for eternal life. Not many of us know of the Bible's origin that we believe makes us right with God through faith in Jesus Christ. And without knowing that history, we are firmly convinced that somehow we are saved. That is something we need to know for sure as it has eternal ramifications.

The Bible, simply put, is a collection of religious texts, writings, or scriptures sacred in Christianity. The Bible takes its name from the **Latin Biblia ('book' or 'books')**, which comes from the **Greek Ta Biblia ('the books')** traced to the Phoenician port city of Gebal, known as Byblos to the Greeks. The Greek word Byblos speaks about the Papyrus plant from which they made paper. It refers to the writing surface used to preserve

God's word. In ancient times, some writers of the Bible used sheep's skin; it took an entire flock of sheep to print the New Testament. In Middle Eastern countries, Parchment, Vellum, Rice Paper, and even Stone Tablets were used to preserve the sacred scriptures we have today.

Moses is the man credited with being the first to preserve God's spoken word for future generations on tablets of stone. When Moses returned from the Mount of God, he had two stone tablets with the word of God inscribed on them by the Lord our God Himself. (see Exodus 20:1-13) God speaks to Moses beginning at the Genesis creation and continuing to the end of Deuteronomy chapter 33, and Joshua writes of Moses death in Chapter 34. The first five books of the Bible are from the breath (finger) of God. Before this time, from Adam to Moses, each generation had what is called an Oral Tradition. We have no record of any word of God in print before Moses wrote. The previous generation would tell the next generation what the Lord our God had said to them concerning the worship of Him. Nothing was preserved in the written word form at this time, just rehearsed verbally.

Bibles in the fourth century (300 AD) were very expensive. One Bible could cost a priest his entire salary for one year. Most people, including many Catholic priests at that time, could not read or write. Until Charlemagne 800 AD, most priests were still illiterate and could not read or write. That is why he began a school to educate the priests so they could effectively preach and teach the word of God.

The Bible's chapters began to be developed in the AD 1200s by a lecturer in Paris. However, the Bible would not fully develop into the chapters we have today until AD 1551.

William Shakespeare quoted from the Geneva Bible five thousand times in his plays. Most early bibles included the fourteen Apocryphal books. Daniel had fifth teen chapters instead of the twelve chapters we have today. One of the King James translators, the Arch Bishop of Canterbury, decreed that anyone who printed a Bible without the fourteen books of the Apocrypha would be fined and imprisoned for 1 yr.

The first Bible printed in America was done in 1663. It was a translation for the Algonquin Indians.

By 400 AD, the Bible was in over 500 different languages, and by 500 AD, there was only one language Latin Vulgate. How did this happen?

In closing, let us remember what Jesus asked His Father in prayer concerning us today. He said, "he was not just praying for these disciples. But also for all those who would believe in Him according to their word." (see John 17:20) Come and journey along with me through history as we discover the origins of how God's Word To Us came to us today.

CHAPTER 1

The Preservation Of And The Corruption Of God's Word

The Preservation Of Gods Word

Moses is the man credited with being the first to preserve God's spoken word for future generations on tablets of stone. When Moses returned from the Mount of God, he had two stone tablets with the word of God inscribed on them by the Lord our God Himself. (see Exodus 20:1-13) Over forty days, God speaks to Moses beginning at the Genesis creation and continuing to the end of Deuteronomy chapter 33, and Joshua writes of Moses death in Chapter 34. The first five books of the Bible from the breath (finger) of God and inscribed on stone by God Himself have been preserved.

Ezra assembles the 39 books of the Old Testament in the fourth century BC between 400 and 301 BC, and the Old Testament scripture Canon (standard) is closed down. The Greek Septuagint (Old Testament) was also excepted at this time as God-breathed.

What was going on in the world at this time? And what was happening in Christianity that would lead to the formation of the Catholic Church and the Bibles we have today? Like most things, it all starts with one man.

The Centralization Of The Church

It is nearly two hundred years from the start of Christianity, and Christianity has spread throughout the Roman Empire.

At this time, each Church from city to city and country to country has its customs and practices of the Christian faith. However, they all share one thing in common, and that is the communal meal. Today we call it Holy Communion or Mass (Eucharist). In those days, they would all come together to share in a banquet of food and fellowship; this was one of the two ordinances the Lord Jesus gave us to observe until he returns. Those again being the Lord's Supper (communion) and Baptism (Immersion in the water where possible). Many in that day who often did not have enough food early on began to think of God and heaven as a place of plenty. Let us remember these people were coming out of a pagan society that was polytheistic (believers in many gods), and now they have cast off their beliefs in the many gods for faith in the one true and living God who supplies all their needs. They were beginning to understand how God relates to us. But it wasn't the theology that came; first, it was the food.

As we see in the book of Acts chapter two (see Acts 2:46), this would lead to an entirely different power structure in the early Church versus the one we see today. In the early church structure, most house churches back then were pastored by women. The householder would be the person who would pastor the Church in their house (see Romans 16:3-5 & 1st Cor 16:19). Women in the Gentile world could own property, unlike Jewish women who by Jewish law could not. (see Acts 9:36-37 & Acts 16:13-15) In a domestic space, men were quite comfortable with women being in positions of authority. Women leaders in the early Church marked the great diversity of the growing Church. However, Christian customs and practices still varied from city to city and country to country and house church to house church. The Church continues to grow, but some see this diversity in Christianity as a threat. There is a move afoot to consolidate all these house churches in a town under one central authority, a person in the form of a Bishop. The church leaders are about to institute a new ordained office in the Church.

Christianity is still undergoing persecution throughout the Roman Empire, and many feel a united front is needed if the new religion is to survive. At the forefront of this movement is a man named Ignatius of Antioch. In 110 AD, he was arrested during the Christian persecutions and transported to Rome to be executed for his Christian beliefs. On his way to Rome, he is allowed to visit some Christian House churches, and after these visits, he begins a movement to bring all those House churches in a town under one person, a bishop, as was previously mentioned. Later on, this position (Bishop) would become a third ordained office in the Catholic Church's hierarchal system. Remember, Jesus Christ gave us two ordained offices, those being preacher and deacon. With this proposal by Ignatius, the office of Bishop gets added. Let us remember Jesus Christ did not authorize this office, but the Catholic Church created it. So the Catholic Church in the coming future would have these three ordained offices bishop, priest, and deacon.

Later the Catholic (universal) Church will be called the spouse of Christ and the Pope Christs' vicar on earth. He will become a god-like figure to Catholics. Protestants, however, will only recognize the two offices previously mentioned as ordained offices. In

Protestantism, Jesus Christ holds the office of the Pope (leader of the Christian Church on earth) and is over every pastor and member.

I believe that Ignatius of Antioch had good intentions in mind for the centralization of the Church, and I don't think he had any evil intent in his heart when he proposed this structure for the Church. However, I don't believe he had any idea just how bad this idea would turn out to be in the future. This Idea of one universal Church under one man on earth is about to be born. It will be called the Holy Roman Catholic Church. This newly created office of the Bishop would eventually become the office of the Pope or Pa Pa (a name used by African Christians to describe their Bishop). From these beginnings, a Catholic hierarchical church administration system would develop from that day and remains with us till this day. Ignatius proposes a church governing structure based on a Roman city. The city becomes the congregation, and the Bishop becomes the Roman administrator. And in this way, every early Church comes to resemble a Roman municipality in the empire of Christianity.

He then writes letters to the churches recommending that Christians "follow the Bishop as Jesus Christ did the Father. To honor the Elders (priests) as they would the Apostles and to respect the deacons as you would the law." He also wrote, "he who is in league with the bishop is in league with God, and he who acts without the knowledge of the bishop is in league with the devil." From this time and from now on until 1517 AD, Christianity will be led by Imperial Rome thinking.

Rome does not permit women to hold leadership positions, so women now lose their power in the Church, and Roman Christianity will demote them accordingly.

The Rise Of Constantine

The effect of Roman culture on Christianity has a tremendous impact on Christian thinkers like Justin Martyr, Origen, Clement of Alexandria, and others. They apply classical Greek logic and philosophy in an attempt to understand God. The 4th century became known as the Golden Age of theology. The theologian Tertullian explains his theology to some Roman philosophers like this. "God made this universe by his word reason and power. Your philosophers also agree that the maker of this universe seems to be the Logos, that is, word and reason. This word we have learned was produced by God and therefore is called the Son of God."

Theology uses Greek philosophy to understand the truth about God and how he relates to us humans and all creation. It had become abundantly clear after the year 200 AD that Christian thinkers would use Greek philosophy to understand the truth about God. That meant the search for the truth of God would become more important than the worship, the love, and the practice of the Christian religion. In their efforts to find out the truth about God, they neglected to live for God in history.

The new faith continued to grow and expand and make inroads into the Roman society. Many slaves, the upper classes, and some Roman Senators were now coming into the Church. More and more, the leaders in the Church were coming from the Roman local elites and city councils. Christianity had bought into the political and social status quo.

The rise of Christianity in just 300 years is one of the most extraordinary success stories in history. It has risen from being a supposed Jewish sect to a Greco-Roman religion spread throughout the Roman Empire. It has grown from a small group of dedicated followers of Jesus Christ to multitudes of Christians throughout the Roman Empire. The story of the growth and spread of Christianity is a highly improbable story but a true one. Christianity has not only survived the Roman persecutions, but it has thrived under them.

In 285 AD., Diocletian decided to divide the Roman Empire into two halves, the west, and east Roman Empire, to make it easier for him to rule over and prevent his rivals from rising against him. It was called a tetrarchy. In the west and east halves of the Empire, there would be an Augustus and a Caesar. Four in all. You can easily see the potential for conflict.

In 312 AD, the failing power structure of this new tetrarchy collapses. A former soldier named Constantine is named Caesar of the West assigned to the furthest reaches of the Western Roman Empire, the English city of York. From there, he marches his legions South across the European continent toward Rome, intent on overthrowing the Western Augustus Maxentius. Eight miles outside Rome, he pauses at the Milvian bridge on the eve of what will be the greatest battle of his military career. While contemplating the fight of his life, he is confronted with that outlawed Christian symbol, the Christian cross. In a vision, Constantine looks into the sky, and he sees a sign of the cross on the face of the sun, and he hears a voice say to him that you are to conquer in this sign. He believes, obeys the word he heard, tells all of his soldiers to paint the sign of the cross on their shields, and into battle they go. He then orders his men into battle under the sign of the forbidden cross, and the victory is theirs.

After winning this great victory in the sign of the cross, Constantine now rewards the Christian faith by signing into law what is called the Edict of Milan (the ending of Imperial persecution of the Church by Rome) in 312 AD. Christianity has now conquered the Roman Empire.

In 323 AD, Constantine marched against the Eastern Augustus, the pagan Licinius, and defeated him in battle after two years of war. Now Constantine was named the sole ruler of both the Eastern and Western Roman Empire in 325 AD. The ceremonies to celebrate the reunification of the Empire is Christian. Many scholars still debate to this day and wonder did Constantine accept Jesus Christ as Savior and Lord that day at the Milvian bridge or Apollo the Sun god? While it is true he was very kind to Christians; it is also true that he maintained some of his paganism. For instance, the Roman coinage still carried the image of Apollo, the Sun god. He changed the day of Christian worship from Saturday, the Hebrew Sabbath day, to the Roman day of the sun Sunday. The question still exists to this day. Did Constantine become a Christian, or was he just a shrewd pagan politician that used Christianity to further his ambitions?

It was common knowledge that Constantine stated that he would not be baptized a Christian until he was on his death bed. Historical records say that Constantine did get baptized just before his death, around 337 AD.

In Constantine's mind, there must have been the thought of one God, one Kingdom, and on earth one Emperor of the East and West who could control the whole thing. And there is over here this religion which has withstood persecution and has one God and one baptism, and in Constantine's mind, this made sense, as it is in heaven, so it must be on earth. One Empire and one Emperor, Constantine and Christianity will serve each other well.

Now the New Testament church under Emperor Constantine turns its attention to creating a Bible. Before this time, there were no twenty-seven documents called the New Testament. From Church to Church and city to city and country to country worship services and the books they studied varied. They had the Apostle's gospels, epistles, and the non-apostolic Gnostic gospels as well. And a book of ethics called the Shepherd of Hermes and the letters of Clement, a follower of Paul the Apostle (see Philippians 4:3). When Emperor Constantine came to power, he wanted to bring them all together in one book. The work on the twenty-seven New Testament documents begins when Constantine decides to sponsor the printing of 50 large Bibles. To Constantine, nobody would say they have not even thought about compiling the Bible into the 66 books we know today.

The champion of Nicea, the North African Bishop Athanasius, and his team are tasked with this responsibility. In AD 367, he lists the contents of the New Testament books from Matthew to the Revelation, and they are the same twenty-seven documents we call the New Testament today. Athanasius is named the champion of Nicea because of his successful defense of the deity and humanity of Jesus Christ at the Nicean council called the Arian Controversy. I believe it would be good for the reader to understand the mindset of some during that time and the alternative views some held about Christ at that time. Also, this intellectual attack would force the Church to define itself to the world, leading to our Christian Creed and the compiling of the sixty-six book Bible we have today.

One of these Gnostics named Arius becomes responsible for what will later be called the Arian controversy. Arius argued because Jesus is called the Son of God, he cannot be equal with God. Arius portrays Jesus as being less than God but more than man. His opponent Athanasius a North African bishop, disagrees with him and maintains that Jesus Christ is of the same essence and substance as God the Father. He is entirely God and fully man. However, this division in the Church is antithetical to Constantine's view of a unified Roman Empire. He calls for the first of seven Ecumenical councils spanning from 325 AD to 787 AD to discuss this question and heal these breaches in the Church. Constantine decides it is time for the Church to produce a definitive statement concerning the Nature of God and the Son (Jesus Christ) for all of Christendom. In the beginning, this meeting was initially called to decide on a day to celebrate Easter. However, after this meeting of Bishop's is over, Christianity will have not only a day to celebrate Easter but a Christian Creed and a sixty-six book Bible as well.

One can only imagine what went through the minds of the bishops who had survived persecution. Now they are invited or ordered to come to hot seaside Nicaea (Modern day Turkey) with all expenses paid by the Emperor. If you were a bishop who managed to live through the Roman persecutions and now the Roman Emperor himself is calling/ordering all bishops to come to Rome, you could give one room for much pause and concern. But when the Emperor called, you came. They may have believed they were all called there to be exterminated at one time. The Bishops don't know it at this time, but Constantine has to depend on them to unify Christianity and, at the same time, the Roman Empire. In Constantine's mind, So goes the Church, so goes the Empire.

At issue is the division in the Church over the nature of Christ. These arguments get down to every letter in a verse of scripture. This giant-sized argument came down to the smallest of the Greek alphabet letters. Athanasius said that Jesus was homoousios (meaning the same substance and essence of God), and Arius said that Jesus was homoiousios (like the same substance). The smallest Greek letter, the iota, decided the difference between the two. They met and discussed, argued, and debated, and they concluded that Arius and his group had it all wrong and Athanasius and his group had it right. Arius and his Church were banished and shut down, and the Christian Creed is written to finally define what Christians believe about the nature and person of Jesus Christ. This Christian Creed still holds to this day.

Christian Creed Created In Nicaea in 325 AD,

We believe in one God, Almighty Father,
Maker of all things seen and unseen,
And in one Lord Jesus Christ, the Son of God,

Begotten of the Father and only begotten,
That is, from the essence of the Father,
God from God, Light from Light,
True God from True God,
Begotten not made,
Of one substance with the Father
Through whom all things were created,
both the things in heaven and the things on the earth,
Who for us men and for our salvation,
Descended and became flesh and became a man,
Suffered and arose on the third day,
and ascended into heaven,
and is coming to judge the living and the dead.
We also believe in the Holy Spirit.

Now that the Church has a creed, it turns its attention to compiling the twenty-seven books of the New Testament. Before any book could become a part of the 27 books we call the New Testament today, they had to fit these four criteria.

1. It had to be written by someone with first-hand knowledge or by someone who received their account from someone with first-hand experience, like Luke, the writer of the Book of Luke.

2. It had to be ancient. Meaning it goes back to the beginnings of historical Christianity AD 30.
3. Could not be local but widely accepted through-out all Christendom.
4. Could not be heretical. Meaning it could not disagree with already clearly revealed Christian teachings or practices.

That is why none of the fourteen Apocryphal books made it into the Bible because they did not meet these four criteria. The 14 Apocryphal books were added for instruction but were not taken as Holy Writ (the inspired word of God) until 1885 AD.

Far away from Rome, Christianity will continue to evolve. Three hundred years have passed, and Christianity now has an Empire, a Creed, and a Bible. In AD 397, the Senate Of Carthage declared the twenty-seven documents complied by Athanasius and his group of scholars in 367 AD to be the New Testament we have today. Do we believe this is God's word because they said so? No! Don't forget what God said and what Jesus Christ prayed (see John 17:20). As Christians by faith, we believe what God's word says to us in 2nd Timothy 3:16-17, and again in 2nd Peter 1:20-21, and my prayer is that you do too.

Christianity had bought into the political and social status quo. Without Christianity having bought into a hierarchy, many modern-day scholars wonder if the Christian religion would have survived if it had not. One historian asked these interesting questions. "At what cost did Christianity buy into political power? At what cost did Christianity buy into hierarchy? At what cost did it compromise some of the values of Jesus to survive as a religion?" The answer to that question will play out over the next 1200 years in the Roman Catholic Church.

The Corruption Of God's Word

Once the Roman Emperor became Christian, so did the Roman people.

Christianity becomes the dominant religion throughout the Roman Empire. There is only one Christian church denomination forming at this time, and it is what we call today the Roman Catholic (Catholic meaning universal) Church. For the next 1200 years, the Catholic church will hold an autocracy of spiritual knowledge and secular knowledge over all Christendom and those living within its sphere of influence. In 400 AD, the scriptures had previously existed in over 500 different languages. However, the Catholic church leaders viewed this as a threat, so in 382 AD, they enlisted the services of a scholar named St. Jerome to translate the Bible into Latin Vulgate and all other books of education. And so, by 500 AD., the Bible gets reduced to only one language, Latin Vulgate.

The majority of the people living at that time had an oral tradition of communication and learning, leaving many in the Roman populace illiterate, unable to read or write. The church would take full advantage of this liability of the masses. From now on, the church would tell them what the Bible said, and they would not need to read it for themselves. They would have to trust their local priests to teach them the truth about what God's word said and how they were to live it out. Many could not read for themselves, and those who could read were not allowed to read God's word for themselves because that would soon come to be called an act of heresy.

After Jerome completed his work, the Catholic church leaders proceeded to ban all other books and Bibles not authorized by the church. If you were caught teaching the Bible unauthorized by the Catholic church, you could be found guilty of heresy and face being burned at the stake as a heretic. Only someone authorized by the church now could administer the blessed sacraments, communion, and baptism or teach the scriptures to someone. You could not even read the Bible to your children at home or rehearse with them the Lord's prayer in English or whatever your native language was. The church would now administer all preaching, teaching and communion, and baptismal services. The local church becomes a salvation station meaning you can only come to Christ through someone authorized by the Catholic Church. The Catholic church wanted to control the people, and how do you do that? By controlling their religion and their education?

The year is 1517, and a German priest named Martin Luther is appalled by selling indulgences to wealthy people. It was, in fact, salvation at a cost for those who could afford it. For him, this was the straw that broke the camel's back. The Catholic church was trying to raise money to pay for the work at the Vatican, so the church allowed local bishops to put indulgences on sale for anyone who could afford it. This move, however, without saying it was for the wealthy because most of the people were poor farmers and could not afford the cost to buy-in. An indulgence was a certain amount of money that one paid for forgiveness from temporal sins in place of penance, which was the Catholic church's teaching at that time. Individuals were buying them instead of taking a pilgrimage or showing other evidence of remorse.

Here is a list of Tariffs Established By Pope John 22nd, first published by Pope Leo 10, that the church created for the people to consult concerning the cost of purchasing indulgences for the forgiveness and the absolution of the temporal sins (sins after baptism) they committed.

For robbing a church, $2.25
Burning down a house $2.75
Kill a layperson $1.75
Forgery or lying $2.00
Eating meat on-lent $2.75 Ravishing a virgin $2.00
Striking a priest $2.75
Robbery $3.00
Priest keeping a mistress $2.25
Procuring an abortion $1.50
The murder of parents $2.50
For absolution of all crimes, $12.00

St, Augustine found it a "necessary evil" in the 5th century to hire 100,000 prostitutes for the priesthood to raise money for the work being done on St. Peters Basilica. The doctrine of celibacy had not been enacted at this time.

Here are some other doctrines the Catholic church taught as well. Several of these teachings will turn out to be the reason Martin Luther, in the end, breaks with the established Church in Rome and becomes the leader of a powerful Protestant Reformation Movement. Before we go forward, let us remember, Jesus Christ gave His church only two ordinances while He was here on earth to observe. Those being Baptism and the Lord's Supper or Communion. Please note that Jesus Christ did not attach any saving efficacy at all to either of these ordinances. He instructs us to observe them as a symbolic practice until he comes to get us, and we return with Him to heaven.

1. **The Sacrament of Baptism is the initiatory rite.** The church taught that original sin and all acts of sin committed up to baptism get forgiven. Infants began to be subjects of baptism in the second and third centuries, and sprinkling became the general mode of baptism by the ninth century. The thinking behind this practice was a little water is as good as a lot.

2. **The sacrament of confirmation** claims to impart the Holy Spirit. The scriptural claim for this process is found in Acts 8:17, 19:6, they say. In the western world, only a Bishop could administer this sacrament. It was conferred shortly after baptism; then, the time

changed to allow the subject to reach their twelfth or thirteenth year until the thirteenth century.

3. **The sacrament of penance** provides for sins committed after baptism. The congregation made the earliest confessions of sin in public, but this practice could not continue for obvious reasons. The worship service would end up being nothing but a revelation of sin service.

4. **The Sacrament of Mass** (the Lord's Supper) or called by the Catholic church, the unbloody sacrifice of the body and blood of Jesus Christ himself. They claimed that the bread and wine, through transubstantiation, turned into the actual body and blood of Jesus inside you. And for this theological reasoning, the Catholic church decided that the laity did not need the wine because they would get all they required in the bread alone.

5. **The sacrament of extreme unction**, is as the name indicates, the last anointing. Its practice gets based on James 5:14. In the administration of this sacrament, the priest anoints the eyes, ears, nose, lips, palms of hands, and feet to get rid of any sins contracted by any of these body parts. A total indulgence is grated but does not take effect until the death of the subject.

These corruptions and many more had also entered into the very word of God. How did this happen? Through unfaithful recopying of the Bible manuscripts over the years. Jesus gave us two ordinances to observe, and now we have seven (two not mentioned here), and they have had a saving efficacy added to two of them, Baptism and the Eucharist. Under the control of the Catholic church, the time from AD 400 to AD 1517 would come to be called the Middle and Dark Ages. Holy Wars break out all over Europe. Pope Leo 10 states, "how profitable this fable of Christ has been to us." With the leaders of the church thinking like that, no wonder that time was called the Dark Ages. At this time, there are two Popes, Clement in France and Urban in Rome. And they are both threatening each other with ex-communication.

But all of this is about to change with a hammer stroke and with the nailing to the church's door at Wittenberg Martin Luther's ninety-five thesis (arguments against Catholic church doctrines) on the eve of All Saints Day, Wednesday, October 31st, 1517. Change is on the way. It has taken 1250 years to get here, but reform is finally here.

CHAPTER 2

The Reformation Of The Church Begins

However, while the Catholic church is doing all it can to consolidate its power and control over the church and state, far away from Rome on a Northern Scottish Isle called Iona, a man named Columbo has started a Bible college. In the fourth century, an underground society has formed at this school called the Culdee's (meaning certain stranger). Joseph of Arimathea, the Pharisee/Disciple who allowed Jesus Christ to have his tomb that no man had ever lain in, left Jerusalem after the death of Jesus. He traveled to Glastonbury, England, and it was there he joined this underground group and became a Culdee himself and built the first above-ground Christian church in Glastonbury, England, the ruins of which are still with us to this day.

This underground society of Christians would preserve the scriptures intact for the next 1200 years; during the Dark Ages, they will resurface again just as they were handed down to us by the Apostles who wrote them. And at just the right time, they will rise again and give birth to what is called today the Reformation Movement.

It's a good thing they did this because the scriptures had been corrupted over the last 1200 years through unfaithful recopying of the Latin Vulgate Bible. Ex-communication (expulsion from the body of Christ), Transubstantiation (the communion bread and wine turn into the literal body and blood of Christ), infant baptism (possessing a saving efficacy), confirmation (confirming the Holy Spirit on the baptized infant in their teens). Reformers will challenge these teachings and others like purgatory (an intermediate place between earth and heaven), indulgences (money instead of penance or to cancel out the penalty for sins), and much more. Reformation of the church and word is coming, but it will not start with Martin Luther, who we credit today with its birth, but he will be the one who brings it to fruition.

In 1300 AD, men like John Wycliff and others began to speak out against the crusades, saying God's word is our guide and not the Pope's word. Pope Uban's call in the twelfth century for Holy War to save Jerusalem from the Muslims in John Wycliffe's mind was not God's will but that of man.

The Crusades

The church and the state are not faring so well at this time. The church has become the plaything of the rich and influential. And the governments are destroying themselves due to the constant warring of the lords of Europe. But just as the Phoenix rose from the ashes, so would the church and the word of God. The church has faced many problems in the past one thousand years and has conquered them all.

In Clairmont, France, in 1095 AD, a new and prominent Pope, Urban the 2nd, comes to power, and he calls for a council of peace to deal with the constant fighting of the lords of Europe. His solution was to harness the aggression of the people of Europe and focus it on achieving a common cause and, at the same time, the goals of the church. Holy war. Urban called for the rescue of Jerusalem from the Muslims. The movement that this call will give rise to will be called The Crusades. He makes this call in a language that he knows the Knights will understand. He sexualized it. He portrayed Jerusalem as a damsel in distress with her purity threatened by the Arab's of Arabia. The response to his call was overwhelming; five armies numbering fifty thousand people showed up. He advises them to wait until they can be adequately provisioned. I do not believe

Urban knew just how many people would show up in answer to his call. He most likely thought he would only get true Knights and Dane's, not all the commoners that showed up.

In the Spring of 1095 AD, having been aroused by persuasive preachers, they set out for the promised land without adequate provisions. Because of this, they begin to loot and pillage as they go to survive — the historical records of this time record many of the atrocities committed by these Christian Crusaders. As they traveled toward Constantinople, the gateway to The East, they wreaked havoc wherever they went. People would direct or miss direct them across their lands as quickly as possible. They were like a plague of locusts. People all over Europe were afraid of them and talking about these people. Even worse, some of them inflamed with imaginations of an entirely Christian world are anti-Semitic, and they begin to say, why do we wait until we get to Jerusalem to slay the infidel? We have infidel in Europe, and they are the Jews.

Despite efforts by local bishops to protect the Jews, they get slaughtered in large numbers by the Crusaders. Three of the five armies are destroyed along the way by angry townspeople who decide to fight back. The two remaining armies finally reached Constantinople, where an anxious Emperor hurriedly ferries them across the Bosporus River to Asia Minor. Once they arrive there, discipline breaks down, and the Turks massacre them. The first crusade turns out to be an unmitigated failure, and the church immediately disowns it. Later it comes to be called "the peasant's crusade."

The second crusade launched in the year 1096 was a crusade of suffering. Although they were true Knights once they got beyond Constantinople, their will to survive and conquer came under severe testing. Finding themselves surrounded by a foreign enemy in a foreign land becomes a test of will, starvation, and death. But they continued their slog until July of 1099 AD, when they finally entered the city of Jerusalem, where a blood bath ensued.

Raymond of Abias wrote, "some of our men were more merciful than others. They cut off the heads of those who were dying while others tossed them into the flames to prolong the agony of their enemies. Piles of hands, heads, and feet were to be seen in the city. Men rode in blood up to their knees and bridle reins. Indeed it was a splendid and just judgment of God." There were too many bodies for the people to clean up. So five months later, when one of the army chaplains arrived, he noted that the whole city stank like an open grave.

The crusaders overnight had turned Jerusalem, a once-thriving populace, into and stinking rotting mess.

Despite all this, the crusades would have an enormous impact on Europe. The people would fight for a common cause for the first time, and a national identity emerged. They began to stoke the flames of trade, and a common currency was born. They created new systems of taxation, and the wealth of the church also began to increase. The crusades were Europe's first collaborative effort as it fought its way out of Barbarism. However, it would come at a high cost. The majority of the populace hated the crusaders, and they left many with a bad taste in their mouths. It has been said that "as we look back from today, one can only conclude that there was nothing even remotely Christian about these disgraceful acts."

It is now the thirteenth century. For almost one thousand years, the Eastern Orthodox Catholic Church in Constantinople has stood the test of time ever since Constantine moved the center of Rome there in AD 330. And for just as long, there has been a division and hatred between the Catholic church's Eastern Greek-speaking and Western Latin-speaking halves. These differences and the greed of one Venetian merchant will culminate in the unthinkable happening. One crusade will go horribly wrong and will result in the sacking of Constantinople by Christian Crusaders.

The year is 1202 AD, and Jerusalem has fallen back into the hands of the Muslims. Pope Innocent III wants to win it back again, so he calls for the fourth crusade. But after a hundred years of crusading, Europe is tired, and not many Knights answer the call. Four hundred miles away is a ninety-five-year-old half-blind crafty merchant named Enrico Dondolo, and he is the governor of Venice. Enrico loves to trade and prefers to do business with the Arabs versus war, and he has not forgotten how he lost his sight one night in a brawl years ago in a Constantinople pub. Enrico agrees to ferry the crusaders across the river, but they cannot afford the cost because not as many knights answered the call to arms as they thought they would. He then asks them to sack one of his maritime competitors, a city named Zara, to get the money they need to pay Enrico. But Zara is a Christian city, and this idea repulses many knights, and they depart. However, the remaining knights conclude that the ends justify the means, and they sack Zara, one of Enrico's maritime rivals. There they become embroiled in Byzantine politics and the cunning of the Venetian Governor. The crusaders restore the Emperor to the throne, and they make a deal with him to bring the Eastern church under the rule of the Western church and provide them with ten thousand knights to join them in their attempt to win back the city of Jerusalem.

When the Emperor fails to deliver the church and the knights, Enrico Dondolo moves to destroy his largest maritime competitor on the Adriatic sea, Constantinople. He convinces the Knights to attack Constantinople, and for three days, they lay siege to the city. And for the first time in one thousand years, the mighty walls of Constantinople fall to its Christian invaders. The Crusaders enter the town and loot, pillage, and rape. They came to the churches, and they stole every valuable thing in sight. Even some clergy are seen taking some of the gold, silver, and other costly artifacts themselves. Pope Innocent III did not know that this would happen when he called for this fourth crusade. He immediately excommunicates all the participants. However, he quickly becomes reconciled to the idea of being the sole ruler of the Eastern and Western halves of the Catholic church. For the next 60 years, Constantinople would remain occupied and would never again reach those heights it had previously enjoyed. Western Christendom would, however, continue to grow. Now you see why

Wycliffe feels the way he does about Urban's call to Holy War.

John Wycliffe had become a member of this underground society called Culdee's as well. The Culdee's have been in operation now for seven hundred years at this time. They had kept the Old Testament uncorrupted in Hebrew and the New Testament in Greek, just as the Apostles and Luke handed down to them. They had the original sixty-six books intact. And now these scriptures are about to resurface, and revival will break out all over Europe. This act will not make the Catholic church happy, and they will do all they can to crush this new movement in its infancy.

John Wycliffe pastored a church in Lutterworth, England, from 1362 to 1372. He wrote a pamphlet called the Wickett, and it is a repudiation of the Catholic church teaching on the doctrine of Transubstantiation. In Wycliffe's mind, Transubstantiation was compared to a pagan sacrifice of Canibal or the cannibalism feast of Baal. It was an old Babylonian custom. He used the Latin phrase Hocus corpus meum to describe it, and that is where we get the phrase hocus pocus. The service had become magical, with the wine and bread magically becoming real inside the person at mass. This act, of course, was not biblical at all, and John Wycliffe called them out on it in his writings and his sermons.

John Wycliffe died in 1384 AD of a stroke while preaching in his church. The Lollard preacher boys carried him out in his chair through the side door, and he was buried there on church property. It is now 150 years before Luther would nail his thesis on the church's door at Wittenburg, and the reformation of the church and the word has begun.

The Catholic church now responds by banning Wycliffe's books and translating the scriptures into the Wycliffe Bible. The Catholic church, 1408 AD at Oxford, also prohibits anyone from translating the scriptures into English or any other language. The only authorized Bible was the Catholic church's version of the Latin Vulgate. In 1428 AD, one hundred and fifty years after the death of Wycliffe, the Catholic church leaders had his bones dug up and burned and then thrown into the River Swift next to his church. They were sending a message to anyone else who thought about doing what Wycliffe did.

John Huss in Checholovokia started reforms there in 1416. He, too, would be tried by the Catholic church and burned at the stake. They used his student's scrolls and books for kindling. He said God would raise someone whose calls for reforms would not be ignored. And those would be his last words. Huss' prophecy would come to pass one hundred years later with a German priest named Martin Luther.

CHAPTER 3

The Restoration Of The Church And The Word

It is now one hundred years later, and the prediction of John Huss is about to come to pass. The year is 1517 AD, Wednesday, October 31st, and a German priest named Martin Luther has become disenchanted with the Catholic's churches sale of indulgences to fund the building of the Vatican in Rome. This act becomes the breaking point for Luther, and he nails his ninety-five thesis of contention on the church's door at Wittenburg. No doubt Luther had his problems with Catholic church doctrine long before this act, but this has become for Luther the straw that broke the camel's back. The previously mentioned corruptions probably had a lot to do with Luthers' sudden disgust with the Catholic churchs' unscriptural teachings.

Whatever the case, the Reformation Movement of the church and Bible have irrevocably begun. Martin Luther has become outraged at the excesses of the Catholic church clergy. There has been a sale announced of indulgences by the bishop of Mainz to fund the work on St. Peters in Rome or Vatican City. It is salvation at a price for those who can afford it, as we have previously mentioned. Luther is reviled for dealing a blow that will irreparably tear apart the one Holy Roman Catholic Church.

How do you hold together a country like Europe? With one common faith, Christianity. That is why the church retaliated against anyone they viewed as trying to tear the Catholic church apart with such ferocity. They believed if there were divisions in the church, this could endanger the church and state. What Luther has started with his ninety-five thesis will give his movement its name, Protestant. By protesting against the excesses of the Catholic church, the Protestant church was born and is still with us to this day. Any church that is not Catholic is Protestant. As Luther continues reading the word for himself, he finds even more reasons to question Catholic teachings. Luther writes the Bible in German, and he also begins publishing works that are sharp criticisms against the Catholic church's teachings. He later comes to call the Pope the Antichrist. You don't need that much imagination to know how the established Church in Rome received these attacks, writings, and words concerning the Pope from Luther.

Pope Leo the 10th issues an edit condemning dozens of Luther's works and gives him 60 days to recant. Luther's response is characteristically Luther. Luther's response, " the papal bull is the sum of all impiety, blasphemy, ignorance, impudence, Hypocrisy, and lying; in a word, it is Satan and his Antichrist." Not surprisingly, Luther gets excommunicated for his response, but he must have a trial by German law. For this, they look to Charles the 5th, the German Emperor.

We celebrate America's independence from tyranny every 4th of July. For the protestant Christian, our independence day from the tyranny of the Established church in Rome is April 17th, 1521. That is the day Martin Luther delivered a ten-second speech that would irrevocably sever the One Universal Catholic Church almost in two. Luther's trial would take place in the German city of Worms. Luther receives one final chance to recant. And Luther once again, his response is correct and in keeping with his character, "unless the scripture convinces me I neither can nor will I recant anything since it is neither right nor safe to act against conscience. God help me."

With that, Luther has been declared an outlaw. And leaves the diet of Worms and becomes a man with no rights at all. This moment is a very uncertain time in Luthers' life because he could be killed, and no one would be held responsible for his death because he's an outlaw. But one of his friends kidnaps Luther and hides him out in his castle in Wartburg, Germany, and there Luther remains hidden for the better part of a year. The reformation of the church has irrevocably begun. Once people find out that they can read for themselves, interpret what they have read, and apply what they have learned to their everyday lives, there is no going back to the old order of things. From that day and from now on, things will never be the same as they had been for just over twelve hundred years of Christianity.

What was central to Martin Luther's newfound faith was that a person could only be made right with God by accepting Jesus Christ as their Lord and Savior. He cited Habakkuk 4:4 and Romans 1:17 for his newfound faith, "the just shall live by their faith." But if it is as Luther says that salvation comes through faith in Christ alone, one could ask, why should I do this and not that since all my sins are forgiven through faith in Christ's death, burial and resurrection? For the Protestants, salvation is not about doing good works or penance or their relationship with the Catholic church. But now, as Luther would have it, salvation can only come through faith in what Jesus Christ has done for all of humanity. And with that teaching, the scriptures all agree.

By the mid fifteen hundreds, almost all of Europe embraced Martin Luther's turn to the individual called Protestantism. A new class of people will be created by this move, which is still with us today, called the middle class. These are people who claim the middle ground between the rich and the poor. Protestantism is spreading all across Europe at breakneck speed. The fact that this is happening shows that the time was right for it. The seeds and the seething were there. It was as if the people were waiting for it the way they flowed into it. Others will now take up the mantle and call for reforms of the word of God as well.

On the foundation of John Wycliffe and others, Martin Luther has begun the reformation of the church. And now, there will also be a restoration of the word. Let us remember the words of Jesus as recorded in the Gospel of John Chapter seventeen and verse twenty. (see John 17:20) He asked his Father in heaven not only to bless those who were under His voice there that day. But also all those who would believe in Him according to their word. Meaning the Bible books they would write, which today we call the New Testament.

As we have seen, the Latin Vulgate over the passing years had been corrupted and no longer communicated God's true intentions. The prayer of Jesus Christ back in

AD 30 on the eve of His crucifixion brought to pass the restoration of His accurate word. Without that, people could not be saved. Salvation is a gift to us from God, and that means no amount of religiosity or works can accomplish that for us. A simple faith in the death, burial, and resurrection of Jesus Christ is the only way to be saved. It was confirmed during the times of Christ and His disciples/Apostles, and it remains the truth to this very day. (see Acts 4:12). A reformed church now needs a restored Bible, and one is one the way. The Catholic Churches' Latin Vulgate corruptions need to be removed, and the accurate word of God recovered and disseminated to the masses.

The year is 1455 AD, and Johannes Gutenberg is about to change the world and Christendom very literally by creating the first movable type printing press. Two men Peter Shafer a wealthy man, and John Faust, aid Gutenberb in this process. Until the printing press's creation, whatever you wanted to preserve in writing had to be written down by hand on mediums like parchment, vellum, rice paper, sheepskin, or stone, as God did for Moses. One copy of the Old Testament on sheepskin would stretch out five hundred feet long. John Wycliffe took ten months to translate his reformation English Bible. With the advent of the printing press, Bibles were printed much quicker—days, not months.

One of the first printings is the Gutenberg Bible. A beautiful Bible that is noted for its typography. They used Woodcuts to help the people through imagery to understand what they were reading. Later they would include text footnotes as well to aid the reader in understanding the word. In the late 1490s AD, a professor at Oxford named Linacre went to Italy to study Greek. There he read the Gospels in Greek, and an incredible feeling of frustration came over him. He said, "either this is not the gospel, or we are not Christain." Linacre discovers that the Latin text (Latin Vulgate) is corrupt and no longer conveys the true intentions of God. About this time, a man named John Collett visits a church in Florence, Italy, pastored by a man named Savanah Roland, and he is impressed by the large crowds attempting to get in. Roland was reading the word of God to his audience in the people's language from the original Hebrew and Greek texts. The result was instant revival. They were reading the word to the people and leaving it to the people to interpret for themselves the meaning of the word they had just heard, unlike the Catholic church, the established church in Rome. For the first time in almost 1300 years, they are hearing the unadulterated words of God.

Later, John Collett does the same thing at his church in Oxford, and the results are the same. He also does it in London and achieves astonishing success. Thousands flock to the church to hear for themselves what the word of God has to say to them. After just six months, sixteen to twenty thousand people tried to get in each week to hear the word of the Lord. No one has written a Protestant Bible yet, and the church in Rome has burned Wycliffe's works and others. Those who came to church would take notes on what they heard and take it back to several countries and share it with whomever; at that time, that is how the words of the Bible began to be decimated. The man who will put to pen and paper the word of God in Hebrew and Greek is Erasmus of Rotterdam. You could say that Erasmus was the most intelligent man on earth from a book learning point of view, why you ask because he had read everything in his day that was in print. He now turns his attention to translating the Old Testament into the original Hebrew and the New Testament in the original Greek, not using the Latin Vulgate as his source for scripture as John Wycliffe was forced to do in 1514-1515 AD. But his friends tell him you will not do that here. So he goes to the continent Bazel Switzerland, and there he writes his Hebrew Greek Bible. The restoration of God's word just got a giant boost. Most people today do not know that the King James Bible was not the first Protestant Bible written. As we shall see later in this chapter, the King James Bible was the last to be written during this restoration period. And, of course, the Catholic church leaders condemned his work and set out to destroy every copy they could get their hands on. But all this does is raise people's interest in this forbidden book, and the unadulterated word of God spreads even further. The Erasmus Bible became the primary source for Martin Luther's German Bible, written six years later. And three years after that, William Tyndale's English Bible. Erasmus died in 1536, but his contribution to Christendom is incalculable. Erasmus' dying wish was that every man, woman, and child had their own Bible to read for themselves.

The first English convert to the reformation was Thomas Bilney in 1517. While at Cambridge, Bilney makes his way to a local book shop. There he purchases Erasmus' forbidden Hebrew Greek Bible. Under his covers in his dorm room by candlelight, Bilney reads Erasmus' Greek Hebrew Bible and gives his life to Christ. In first Timothy one fifteen, he reads where Paul said he was the chief of sinners, and Bilney says, no, I am the chief of sinners. (see 1st Timothy 1:15) He was ordained a priest in 1519 and began to spread William Tyndale's English Bibles and other forbidden literature on the campus at Cambridge, and hundreds converted to Christ. One night Bilney shared his confession to Hue Latimer, and Hue Latimer said that he learned more in that one night about faith and salvation listening to Bilney's confession than the ten years he spent at Cambridge.

Bilney gets arrested and is sentenced to being burned to death at the stake. He tells his friends not to worry, saying God will protect him from the heat of the flames. The following day he was burned at the stake, and they used William Tyndale's Bibles as kindling to stoke the fire.

The established church in Rome has done its best to exterminate anyone trying to allow the people to read the word of God for themselves. To them, this is seen as a threat to their power and rule over the people. And every time they take one reformer down, Jesus raises another man or woman to continue the work. And this time will be no different.

CHAPTER 4

The First English Translation Of The Bible

Imagine an English-speaking world without Shakespeare, Tennyson, T. S. Elliott, or C. S. Lewis. They all had one thing in common their contribution to the English language. That is what Christendom would be like without William Tyndale and his thoroughly readable English Bible. It may be surprising that he is not very well known despite his invaluable contribution to Christendom. Let me introduce him to you.

William Tyndale was born in Gloucester, England, in 1494 AD and would be hunted for 11 years of his life before finally being captured by the established church in Rome hired bounty hunter. His only crime was obedience to the call of his God, and this became resistance to tyranny. The tyranny that was being heaped on those who resisted the established church in Rome. Tyndale enrolled at Oxford in 1505, and he literally grew up at Oxford. And in 1515, and earned his master's degree at age twenty-three. Tyndale spoke eight different languages fluently, and no matter which language he was speaking, you would think it was his native tongue. He founded the White Horse Society, made up of twenty-five men. All of which, except one Miles Coverdale, will be beheaded or burned at the stake. During this time, five men and two women are accused of heresy, tried and found guilty, and burned at the stake. Why? Because they taught their children to pray The Lord's prayer in English. This act shows the lengths the Catholic Church would go to maintain power and control over the people/church. The church in Rome has begun hiring bounty hunters to track down and punish all dissenters.

One night while Tyndale was around the table with other priests and Bishops, one Bishop said, "I revere the popes' law more than scripture." William Tyndale could not restrain himself, and he cut loose on that Bishop. To this, Tyndale responds, "I defy the Pope and all his laws. And if God spares my life these many years, I will make it possible for the boy who drives the plow to know as much scripture as you do." After this, Tyndale has come under their suspicions for his views on scripture and his interpretations of them. He is called before a powerful Bishop at that time, and Tyndale is warned to stop his reformative actions or face severe consequences for his actions. Tyndale knows he has to leave there if he is going to print his Bible.

With a strategic plan and help from some friends, Tyndale began translating the Bible into English in 1524. He travels to Wittenberg, Germany, to meet with Martin Luther. After spending some time there, he continues to Cologne, Germany, to print His Bible. The church has hired a bounty hunter named Henry Philips to track down and bring to justice William Tyndale. While Tyndale is at the printers, he is tipped off that the bounty hunter is coming. He quickly grabs his work and runs out the back shortly before Henry Phillips, the bounty hunter, arrives at the front door. He travels by boat up the Rhine River and makes his escape to the German city of Worms. With the help of Peter Shaffer Jr., the son of Peter Shaffer Sr., who helped with the Guttenberg Bible, finances the printing of six thousand of Tyndale's English Bibles. In 1526 they then loaded them on ships bound for England.

Later in 1526, Bishop Tunstall condemns Tyndale's English Bible and sets out to burn everyone he can get his hands on. He even offers to pay for them so he can burn them. He admitted he did not understand what this Bible was all about, but he was sure it was naughty in his own words. What happens instead is the same thing that happened with attempts to get rid of the Erasmus Bible. It just increased the people's interest in it and caused it to spread even further. Bishop Tunstall gave it tons of free publicity. After this time, Tyndale would move from place to place, copying and revising as he went. Tyndale was tired of all the running around and decided in 1533 to settle down. He settled down in an English house in Antwerp.

The bounty hunter hired by the church in Rome, Henry Phillips, tracks down Tyndale, finds him, and befriends him. He is allowed a privilege many would love to have had. He was allowed to look at Tyndale's books other literary works firsthand and up close. After nine years of evading capture by the bounty hunter hired by the church in Rome, Tyndale is finally caught. In the winter months of May of 1535 AD, Tyndale goes out for the night, and while he is passing through a narrow alleyway, his newfound friend Henry Phillips springs his trap, and Tyndale is caught in it and is arrested.

Tyndale will spend the last 500 days of his life deep in the bottom of the Vilvorg Castle at Antwerp. He was tried there and accused and found guilty of heresy. All we know about his time spent in prison comes from a letter he wrote to the King in 1535. Tyndale's request, "I beg your lordship through the Lord Jesus Christ that if I am to remain here through the winter. You will be kind enough to send me a warmer cap from my goods because I suffered greatly from the cold in my head, and I am inflicted with inflammation and congestion. Also, a warmer coat because that which I have is very thin. And above all, I beg your kindness and clemency to have my Hebrew Bible, Hebrew Grammar, and Hebrew Dictionary that I may spend my time with that stuff." Was Tyndale's request granted? We don't know. On October 6th, 1536, William Tyndale was led out to the public square and tied to a pole with a rope around his neck. He is given one last chance to recant. The signal is given when he does not, and the rope around his neck is tightened until he dies. He is then set ablaze with his English Bibles and other literature used as kindling for the fire.

Tyndale's friend Miles Coverdale now prints his Bible. Ninety percent of it is based on William Tyndale's English Bible. The King of England, Henry the Eighth, took it even further. He authorizes the printing of 20 thousand Bibles called the Great Bible. They were to be sent out to every church in England. The Great Bible as well is based on ninety percent of William Tyndale's Bible. The Great Bible has a generous portion of woodcuts to help the people see what they were reading. They also had footnotes in the margins to aid the readers' understanding of the scriptures as well. Having one of these Bibles was akin to being in a class with a Bible teacher. Outside the Bible in the 16th century, books like Fox Book Of Martyr's were also written and filled with woodcuts to give the reader a visual and textual understanding. This book showed how the church in Rome punished its dissidents. King Henry the 8th had removed the church in England from under the control of the established church in Rome. He created what is called today The Anglican Church or Church of England. He wanted a favor from the Pope, but he did not get it, so he left the Catholic church, and The Church Of England was born.

The Rise of the Anglican Church

Most developing nations align themselves with the new protestant Reformers and against the power of Rome. Nowhere is this more evident than in England, where Protestantism was born so that King Henry VIII could divorce his wife. This battle between the church and state will come from Henry VIII, one of the Pope's staunchest allies. The Pope had even given Henry the title "Defender of the faith." But now, in 1533, Henry desperately needs a Papal dispensation to divorce his current wife Catherine of Aragon and marry his currently pregnant Mistress Ann Bolin in a desperate attempt to produce a male heir to replace him on the throne. Of course, this is against Catholic church law.

Henry secretly marries Ann Bolin anyway, but for the child to become a legal heir to the throne, their marriage must have the blessing of the Catholic church. Henry receives word that Pope Clement the 7th in Rome has denied Henry's request. In response, Henry deposes the Arch Bishop of Canterbury and replaces him with his own choice. The new Arch Bishop immediately annuls Henry's first marriage to Catherine of Aragon and recognizes Henry's secret marriage to Ann Bolin. Back and forth goes the argument between church and state.

Finally, the Pope in Rome, Clement VII, excommunicated Henry, and Henry became so angry he broke with the Catholic church in Rome and found what is called today the Anglican Church or the Church of England. He did not stop there in 1534. Henry goes one step further, requiring all his subjects to swear an oath to the Supremacy Act. The Act states that Henry is the supreme ruler in England, placing him above church authorities. "Be it enacted that the King shall be taken and accepted and reputed the only supreme head on earth of the Church of England."

The King now turns his attention to a humanist named Sir Thomas Moore, who is Lord Chancellor. Moore has no illusions when it comes to King Henry VIII. Listen to this quote by William Roper attributed to Thomas Moore. "If my head should win him a castle in France, it shall not fail to go." Thomas Moore has not only refused to attend Henry's marriage to Ann Bolin, but he also refused Henry's Act of succession, making his successors heirs to the throne. Henry has Moore thrown into the Tower of London.

On July 6th, 1535, Thomas Moore was beheaded, dying for his principles, and after all this, Ann Bolin failed to give Henry a male heir. She gets beheaded just eleven months later. Thus friendship is lost. Honor is betrayed. The church of England was born, and Thomas Moore was beatified by the Catholic church 400 years later by Pope Pius the 11th. No longer would the Pope be the supreme authority in Europe. And never again would the Catholic church be the dominant denomination in Western Europe.

In 1553, His daughter Mary came to power, and Queen Mary (Bloody Mary) wanted the church of England to return to the established church in Rome. But many in the populace do not agree with this decision. During her four-year reign of terror, some 3000 people were beheaded or burned at the stake. One of the first men, Henry the 8th, licensed to print a Bible in 1537, John Rogers is one of the first to be burned at the stake. Most escaped to Geneva. Miles Coverdale and John Knox reprint Tyndale's Bible, and they call it the Geneva Bible. Chapters and verses were first introduced by a lecturer in Paris named Robert Stephens in 1550 but would not be fully developed until 1551. The Puritans used this Bible to convert Pocahontas and her people. From 1550 to 1560, one hundred and fifty Geneva Bibles were printed and for 250 years became the Bible of choice of protestant Christians. The Geneva Bible was quoted by William Shakespeare 5000 times, and it was the Geneva Bible that came with the explorers on the Mayflower.

CHAPTER 5

The Kings Jame Bible

In 1604 AD, the Puritans approached King James and requested the printing of an English Bible. He agrees but asks that no notes be placed in the margins, just the word itself. Previous Bible notes in one case described the Pope as being the beast that comes from the bottomless pit as described in Revelation. (see Revelation 11:7) So King James wanting to avoid controversies like that, asked that no notes be included. However, the fourteen Apocryphal books would be. If you remember, these are the books Jerome in AD 400 put an asterisk by because he could not find them in the original Hebrew. But they were kept in for study but not to be taken as the Inspired Word of God.

King James employed fifty scholars learned in Hebrew and Greek for this task. They were divided into six groups, and each group worked on their section. They used the Geneva Bible, William Tyndale's Bible, and the Bishop's Bible as a resource. They also consulted the original Hebrew and Greek, as well as the Greek Septuagint. The compilation of the King James

Bible we know today is about to arrive. This process will take a total of six painstaking years of hard work and effort. They are in no hurry when it is done, they want it to be done once and for all, and they will. They painstakingly styled the English language to make it easy to read and memorize. Over ninety percent of William Tyndale's English Bible has made it into the King James Bible, making the King James Bible the most accurate Bible we have today. It is also the most sought-after Bible in the world. In 1611, King James now ordered the printing of twenty thousand King James Bibles, one for each of the churches in England under his reign. It is God's Book, His story. The most remarkable book from that day to this one that has ever been printed.

The Old Testament at that time included 3 of the Apocryphal books. Daniel had fifteen chapters versus the twelve we have today. The books included were, The Three Children, Bel And The Dragon, and Susanna. Bibles printed before 1885 had 80 books versus the 66 we have today. Every Bible published before 1885 had to include the fourteen Books of the Apocrypha, or the printer could face a hefty fine and one-year imprisonment. Those of us born after 1885 are the first generation to have a Bible free of the fourteen Apocryphal books. The British and Foreign Bible society excluded them after 1885.

The Bible Comes To America

Wars break out all over Europe between Catholic and Protestant Christians. When its believed that diversity is a threat to stability, attempts at resolution often come violently. The church has a civil war that lasts just over one hundred years — called the one hundred years war. Both Catholics and Protestants were vying to be the dominant religion in Europe. And they are very willing to kill for it. These wars finally come to an end out of pure exhaustion. At the cost of many lives and their economies, they decide to allow each other to exist. But and uneasiness will exist between them from that day to this day.

Catholic and Protestant Christianity has spread throughout the Eastern and Western halves of Europe and the Middle East. And now Christian missionaries, both Catholic and Protestant, will take the word of God to both South and North America. The sixteenth-century will become a significant turning point in Christianity for two reasons. The protestant reformation movement and the building of nimble three-masted Portuguese sailing ships enabled travelers to go where they had never gone before. It is the age of exploration, and wherever they go, they take their Christian faith and the Word of God with them to Africa, Asia, and North America.

Christianity has now crossed the Atlantic and has found its way into the North American Colonies through the open-air revivals conducted by both John Wesley and his colleague Gorge Whitfield. The Great Awakening sparked a revival of God's word in the North American colonies and a new shared identity. Most of those who left Europe came to the North American shores seeking freedom from state-run religion and other state and religious oppression. Europe was still a place that did not allow for freedom of choice when it came to faith. Some parts of Europe were more tolerant of non-Anglican and Catholic sects of Christianity, such as the Puritans. But in most cases, as in the past, diversity was viewed as something that would imperil the whole state. Therefore diversity was seen as something not good for the nation.

The first of those groups that would come to North America seeking religious freedoms would be the Puritans in 1607. They are disciples of John Calvin and Oliver Cromwell, and they are English Separatists. They have come to America as a vanguard ahead of those who would follow later. They have come to North America to build a city of God like John Calvin attempted to do in Geneva. Then the King back in England would see how Christianity is supposed to work and adopt puritanism as the new state religion, and they would all be welcomed back as heroes by the King and all the people of Europe. At least that was what they were hoping would happen, but it would not quite work out that way. They did not come to America to create an inclusive free state. Their Separatist views made them no different than those who caused them to leave Europe in the first place. They viewed any deviance from their style of worshiping God as destructive to their idea of what they called the City of God. Other non-tolerant Protestant Christian denominations would also make their way to the North American shores. They would all come with their version and method of worshiping our Lord. Soon the East coast would become a tapestry of Protestant Christian denominations. By the 1700s, the Puritans were in Massachusetts and Connecticut, Presbyterians occupied Long Island, Lutherans were along the Delaware River, Anglicans were in Virginia, and a small Catholic settlement in Maryland. In the late seventeenth century, two men are about to steer North America away from becoming an intolerant country. Their names are Roger Williams and William Penn. These two men will become responsible for making

America the most religiously tolerant nation in the world. It will become the model for the rest of Christendom all across the globe.

Over in England, Roger Williams is one of only eight men to receive a scholarship to Cambridge for his knowledge of Latin, Greek, and Hebrew. Williams is already controversial for his beliefs in freedom of worship. He sets sail for America and arrives on her shores on February 5th, 1631. He preaches in Salem and Plymouth, but his liberal views almost get him deported, for the New World is not yet a place of religious tolerance. Roger Williams once said, "a forced uniformity confounds civil and religious liberty and denies the principles of Christianity and civility. That cannot be a true religion that needs carnal weapons to uphold it. No man shall be required to worship hold or maintain a worship against his will."

In the dead of winter, Roger Williams makes his way sixty miles South to the headwaters of Marigansit Bay. He founds his colony there in modern-day Rhode Island, and he calls it Providence, meaning under God's compassionate (benevolent) care. Roger Williams would have nothing to do with the English Establishment. He cut the English cross out of the flag at one time because he felt Christianity had nothing to do with the King of England.

In 1682 AD, another man set sail for North America, and his name is William Penn. He also has visions of a more inclusive Christianity and country. Out of respect for his late father, the King of England gave him a large tract of land in North America, which he named in honor of his father, Pennsylvania or Penn's Woods. William Penn, like Roger Williams, creates one of the most religiously free colonies in North America. Anyone was welcome in Pennsylvania as long as they worshiped a monotheistic (meaning one God) God. Penn appoints himself governor and drafts a constitution for his new city. Penn made it plain that no one who worshiped the one almighty God would in any way be molested or persecuted because of their religious beliefs. Later on, the ideals of these two men would have a profound effect on the shaping of the laws that would govern the new emerging country called America. Penn's new colony attracts people of all faiths, and it is now that the capital city gets its name Philadelphia the City Of Brotherly Love.

April 19th, 1775, dawn breaks on the Village Common of Lexington, Massachusetts. A ragtag group of Minutemen awaits the arrival of the advancing British Red Coat troops who have come to restore order in the now rebelling 13 colonies. The first shots are fired, and the revolutionary war has begun. America's battle for freedom from Europe's Monarchical rule and taxation without representation has irrevocably begun. This war is also a Christian war of religious liberty versus toleration. For the first time, this war will settle the conflict between the church and the state, which has plagued Christianity as far back as Charlemagne and Pope Leo III in 800 AD. This war will usher in an era when all Christian faiths under one government have equal rights for the first time in Christian and world history.

On October 19th, 1781, British General Charles Cornwallis surrenders to Gorge Washington at Yorktown. Although it's not evident at this moment, America's war for independence is over. Ten years later, in 1791, the new leaders composed the new constitution. It is now that the social models of Roger Williams Providence and William Penn's Pennsylvania now have a profound influence on the framing of the American constitution. All Americans living in the colonies would now be free to worship as they please without interference from the governing authorities. This change made a massive difference from what they experienced in Europe under the Anglican or Catholic churches. For instance, the Anglican church in England would tolerate your denomination but not view it as normative religion. Although without saying it, they were inferring that you had some defect because you were not a part of them.

Religious freedom went far beyond religious tolerance because it did not require the state's blessing to validate them. This peace between church and state would become a model for the rest of the world. It turns out that the decision to take religion out of government produces one of the most religious tolerant governments in the world. It fostered an environment where spiritual Entrepreneurs could vi for the attention of those seeking to belong to a particular church denomination. In a nation with so many different faiths, they cannot single out one as the best one. This practice led to so many of the religious wars they heard about or had experienced in Europe. To avoid plunging their new country into what had plagued Europe for years, they wrote a constitution that would prevent that from ever happening. The drafters have little choice but to protect all religions. This protection becomes the cornerstone of one of this nation's most cherished documents, the Bill Of Rights. It states, "Congress shall make no law respecting an establishment of religion or prohibiting the free exercise thereof" First Amendment U.S. Bill of Rights.

In 1792, the British Embargo began and cut off all shipments of the Bible to the North American Colonies. Maybe this was an effort to demoralize the troops; who knows. During the British embargo, the leaders in America imported Twenty thousand Bibles from Holland and Scotland. The Brown Family Bible is published about this time with the inscription "Sacred To Justice, Liberty, And Peace." With a list of some very influential subscribers. Such as Gorge Washington, President Of The United States, John Jay 1st Chief Justice Of The Supreme Court, who also served as president of the Bible Society, And John Quincy Adams, who also served as the Bible Society President and many others. In 1791 Isaac Collins and Isaiah Thomas published their first Family Bible.

The Protestant Bible has been established as the best-selling book year in and year out for 200 plus years. The Bible has been the best seller for over 350 years in the English-speaking world. Thomas and Collins Bibles would set the standard for Bible publication for more than 110 decades.

Luther and Tyndale rediscovered faith the lost message of the church, giving them freedom from persecution and spiritual starvation. Martin Luther's Church reforms coupled with Tyndale's Bible restoration work have dramatically changed Christendom from that day to this one. Martin Luther's newfound faith says a person could only be made right with God by accepting Jesus Christ as their Lord and Savior. He cites Habakkuk 4:4 and Romans 1:17, "the just shall live by their faith." For the Protestants, salvation is not about doing good works or penance or their relationship with the Catholic church, which taught that salvation could only come through the church. But now, as Luther would have it, salvation can only come through faith in what Jesus Christ has done for all of humanity. We do good works because we are saved, not to be saved. And with that teaching, the scriptures all agree.

Martin Luther's reformed church without a restored Bible would have failed. And Tyndale's restored Bible without a welcoming reformed church would have failed. Luther and Tyndale served each other, and all of Christendom has significantly benefited from this union.

As we think back on the prayer Jesus prayed in John 17:20, it is not a mystery to us as to why Jesus prayed those words. As we passed through history following the word, we saw just how much that prayer Jesus prayed meant. The Devil repeatedly tried to corrupt God's word and prevent us from being saved through faith in Jesus

Christ and what He accomplished for us. That is why Jesus says in 2nd Timothy 2:15 that we should study to show ourselves approved to God and become workmen who are not ashamed and correctly explain God's word. Satan's attempt to keep us from Jesus by corrupting the word failed, and that is why we are saved today. Many scholars still debate and wonder whether those who joined the Catholic church from AD 400 to AD 1500 trusted Jesus for salvation or the established church in Rome's teaching on deliverance? Whatever the case, we have the word today, and just as the Lord said to us in it, we should allow it to guide us in our personal lives, family lives, church life, and civic lives.

A final word. Today, we have many different versions of God's word, and some have said certain scriptures were removed, which changed the meaning of God's word. That is not true. Bible translators have always made an effort to make the Bible easy to read and understand so we can live it out in our daily lives. Just because a scripture may seem to have been left out, a closer look will reveal two scriptures were compounded into one. They do this for clarity and ease of understanding. Remember, not until 1551 AD, was the Bible separated into the chapters and verses we have today. They did this to make it easier to remember not to change the meaning of God's word. So do not be afraid of Bibles that make it easy for us to know and understand what the Lord is saying to us. We do not speak the Kings' English either; we speak American English. Before AD 400, the Bible was already in over 400 Hundred different Languages.

In closing, I am sure there is one Bible version just right for you with all of the versions we have available to us today.

Lord Jesus, Bless the readers of this book to know the truth of your word so that they might proclaim and teach it without reservation. Bless them to be able to provide answers to those who still have doubts. Let your Word To Us become the Corner Stone of all our lives and families lives. In your name, my wonderful, kind, and loving, faithful Lord and Savior, Amen

"All Scripture is inspired by God and is useful to teach us what is true and to make us realize what is wrong in our lives. It corrects us when we are wrong and teaches us to do what is right. God uses it to prepare and equip his people to do every good work. Above all, you must realize that no prophecy in Scripture ever came from the prophet's own understanding, or from human initiative. No, those prophets were moved by the Holy Spirit, and they spoke from God."

"It is impossible to enslave, mentally or socially, a bible-reading people. The principles of the bible are the groundwork of human freedom."

Horace Greeley 1852

NOTES:

69

NOTES:

70

NOTES:

NOTES:

____

72

NOTES:

73

NOTES:

74

NOTES:

NOTES:

76

NOTES:

NOTES:

NOTES:

NOTES:

NOTES:

NOTES:

82

NOTES:

NOTES:

84

NOTES:

NOTES:

NOTES:

NOTES:

NOTES:

89

NOTES:

90

NOTES:

NOTES:

NOTES:

NOTES:

NOTES:

NOTES:

NOTES:

NOTES:

NOTES:

NOTES:

NOTES:

NOTES:

NOTES:

NOTES:

NOTES:

NOTES:

NOTES:

NOTES:

NOTES:

NOTES:

NOTES:

NOTES:

112

NOTES:

NOTES:

114

NOTES:

NOTES:

NOTES:

NOTES:

NOTES:

NOTES:

NOTES:

NOTES:

NOTES:

NOTES:

NOTES:

125

NOTES:

NOTES:

NOTES:
